COCKTASTIC!

First published 2016 by Retro Inc Books
www.retroinc.co.uk
© 2016

ISBN 978-1539874683

Ella Cotton

Flower Cock

Inspired by Jeff Koons giant flower dog sculpture 'Puppy'. Koons is infamous for his adult photographic series 'Made in Heaven' depicting himself and former wife naked and in flagrante.

I couldn't bring myself to illustrate Koons actual willy.

Roman Bell Cocks

These phallic objects protected the ancient Roman household against the evil eye, bringing luck and fertility.

Adorned with bells, these were known as tintinnabula and used as wind chimes.

Michelangelo's David

David is a masterpiece of Renaissance sculpture. Michelangelo was only 26 when he started carving the 17 ft statue and it took him two years to complete.
After its unveiling, the sculpture was given a gilded loin-garland. David is uncircumcised and has very neatly coiffed pubic hair.

It's said that David's penis 'eye' follows you around the room.

Penis Mandala

The mandala is a beautiful image in art and also
great for colouring in.

So I have drawn you a penis mandala.

Robert Mapplethorpe
'Man in Polyester Suit' (1980)

Mapplethorpe's controversial photo of his well endowed lover sold at Sotheby's New York in 2015 for $478,000.
The photo was part of the 'X Portfolio' which had ironically received funding from the National Endowment for the Arts.
It remains one of Mapplethorpe's most enduring images.

Egyptian cock hieroglyph

The phallus has many depictions in Egyptian hieroglyphs.

A symbol of fertility, it is often associated with the gods Min and Osiris.

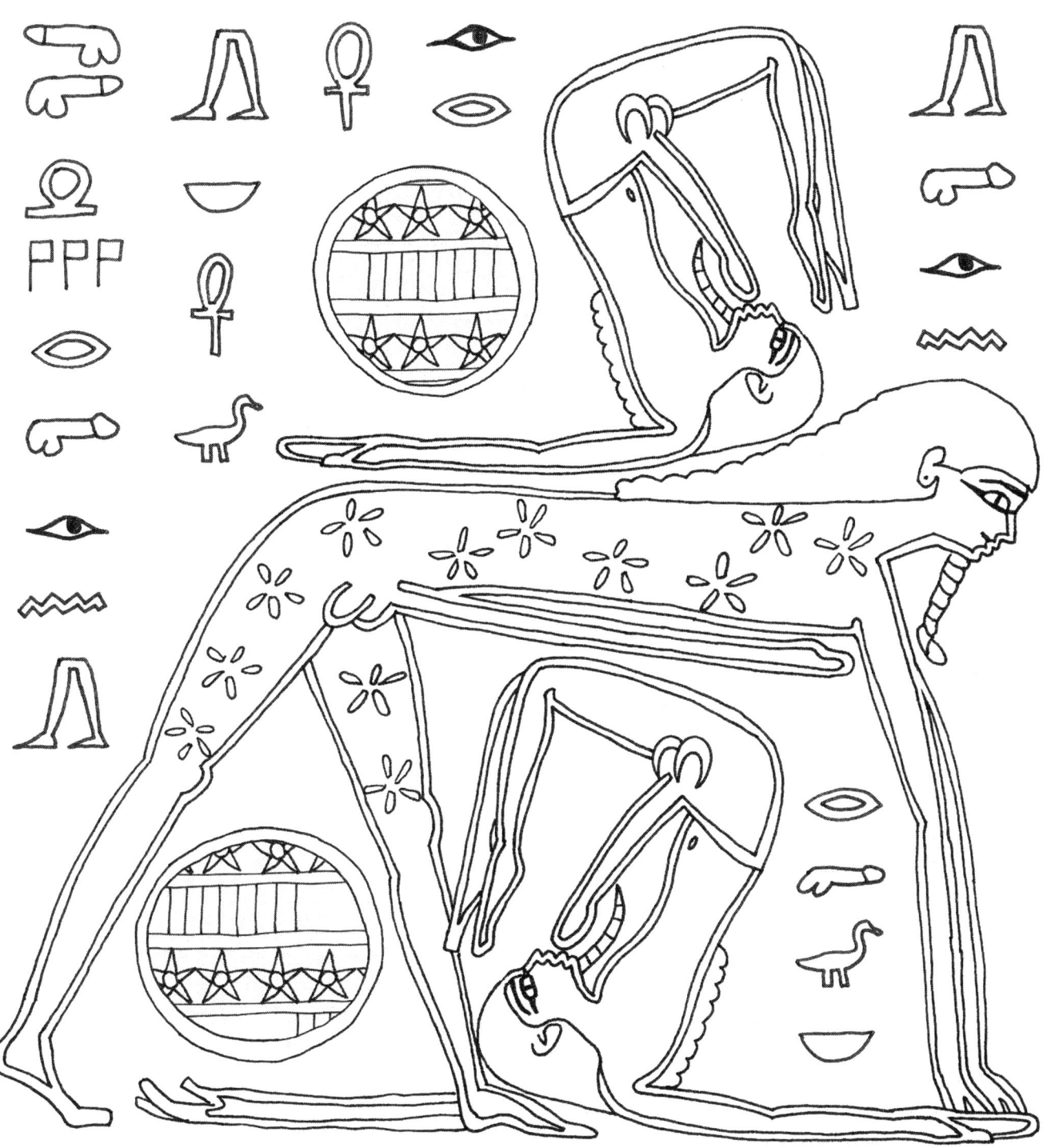

Nuns harvest cock fruit from
the penis tree.

A 14th Century manuscript illustration from
Romance of the Rose by Jeanne de Montbaston.

Jeanne worked with her husband on illuminated
manuscripts in Paris.

Bhutan Cock Dragon

Bhutan has a tradition of phallus mural
paintings adorning houses and buildings.
They are said to drive away the evil eye and bring
good luck.
Wooden phalluses are also pounded into
agricultural fields to bring fertility.
Several monasteries display wooden cocks
to bless.

Marcel Duchamp
'Fountain' (1917)

One of Duchamp's most famous works and an icon of
20th century art.
Duchamp invented found art or the 'readymade'.
In this case, he took a standard porcelain urinal,
signed it R. Mutt and entered it into
Society of Independent Artists.
It was rejected as indecent.
Ironically, Duchamp was head of the exhibitions
hanging committee.

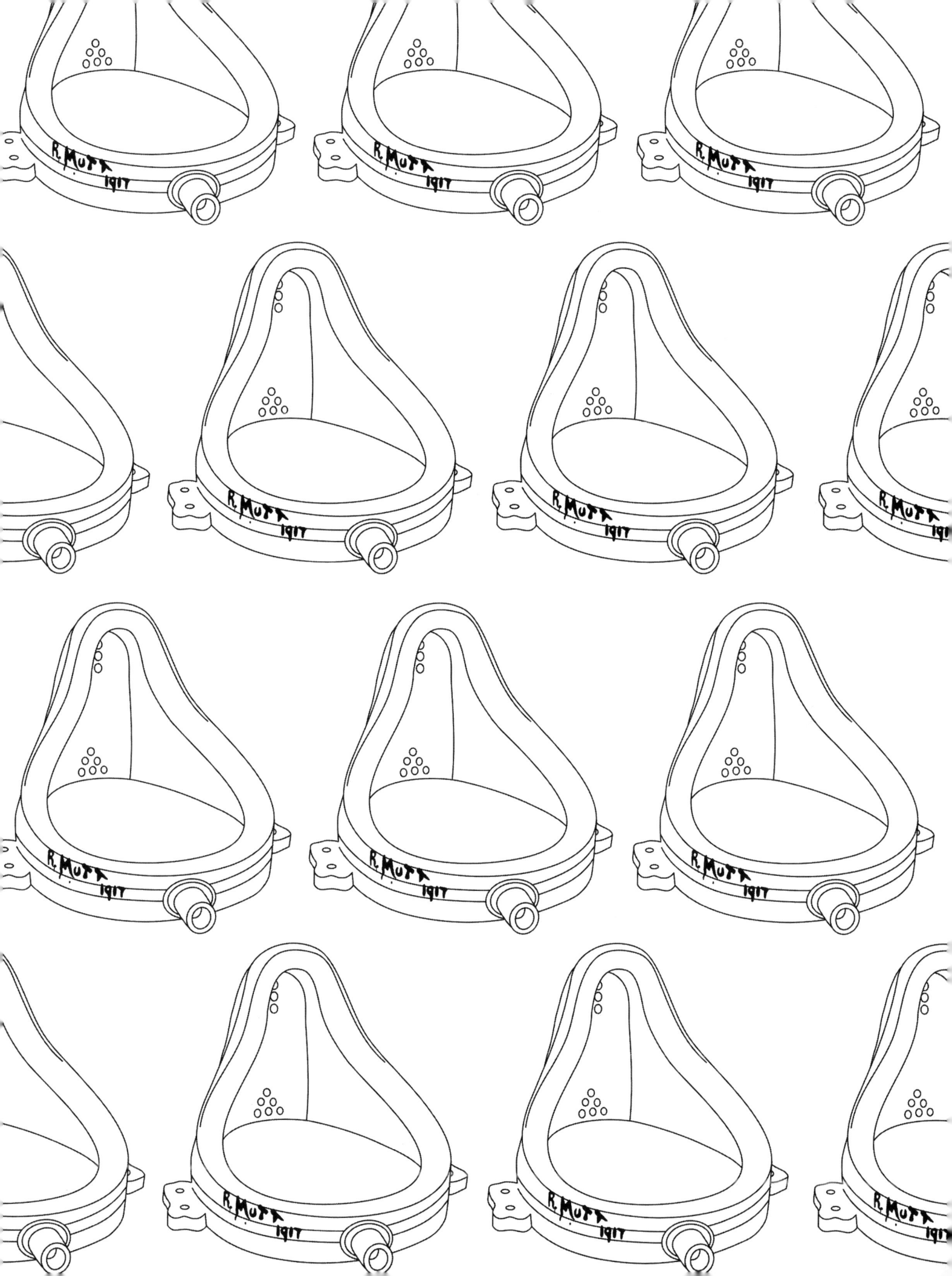

Egypt

Hieroglyphic depiction of the god Osiris.
It is believed that Tutankhamen's body was
mummified with his cock at a 90 degree angle.

The mummified penis has since been broken off
and is missing or stolen.

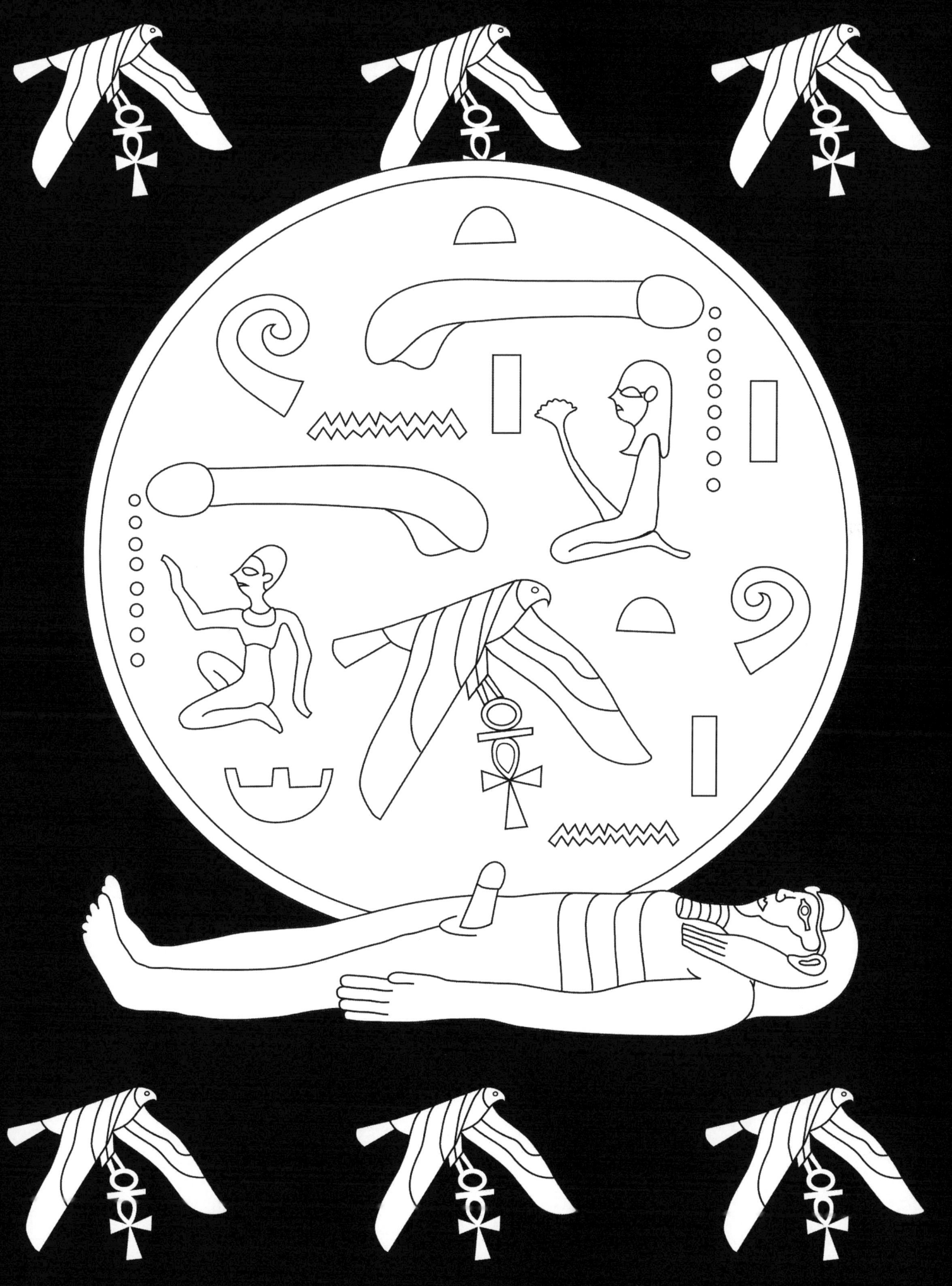

Grecian Urn

The penis was also a symbol to ward off the
Evil Eye in Ancient Greece.
There is a tradition of sexual and erotic acts being
depicted on early Grecian ceramics.

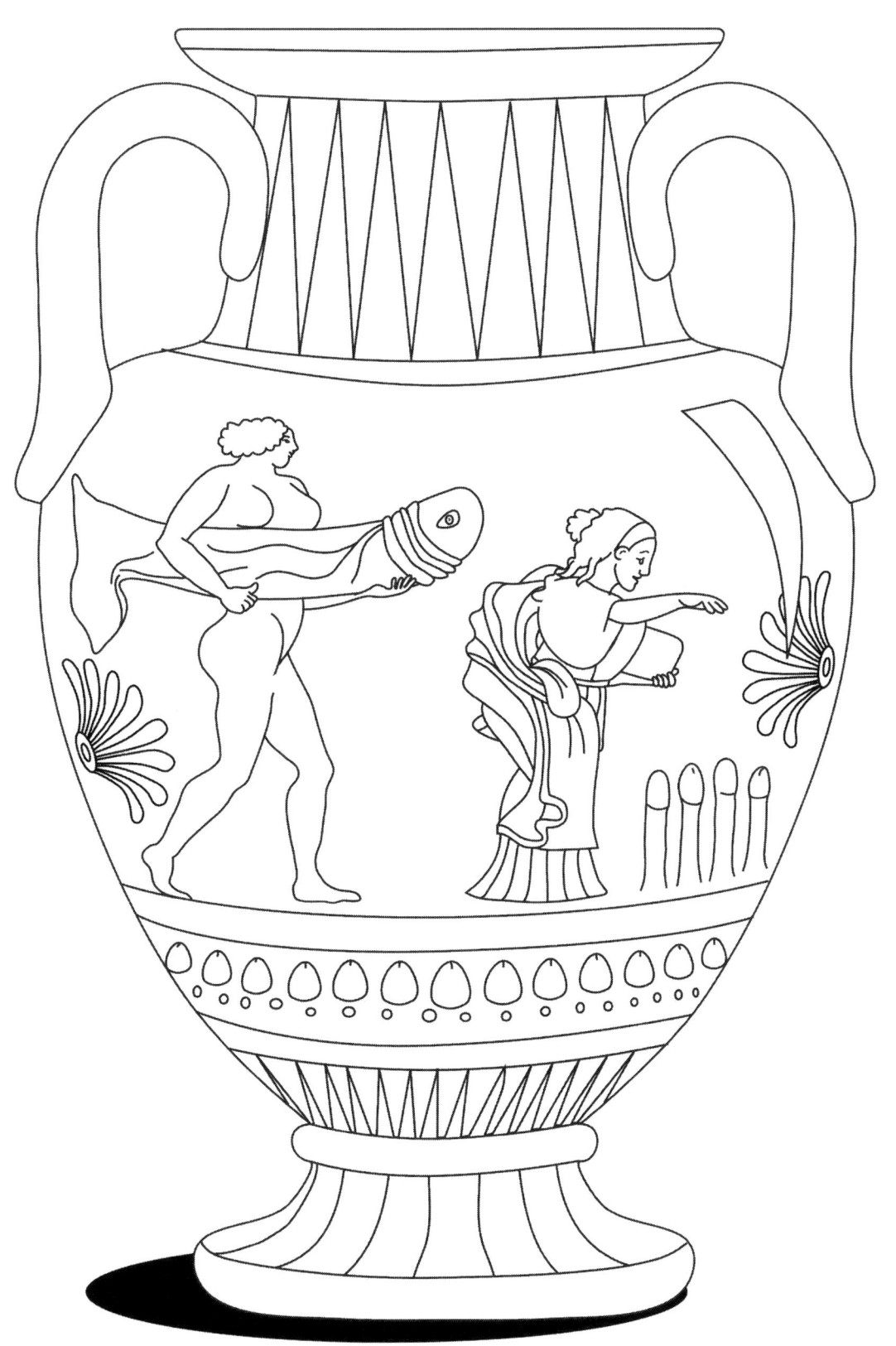

The Penis Park

Haesindang Park in South Korea has a large collection of giant phallic sculptures created by Korean artists.
The park celebrates joy, spirituality and sexuality.

There are penis shaped benches to sit on, and visitors can pay tribute at the temple by leaving small, naughty gifts.

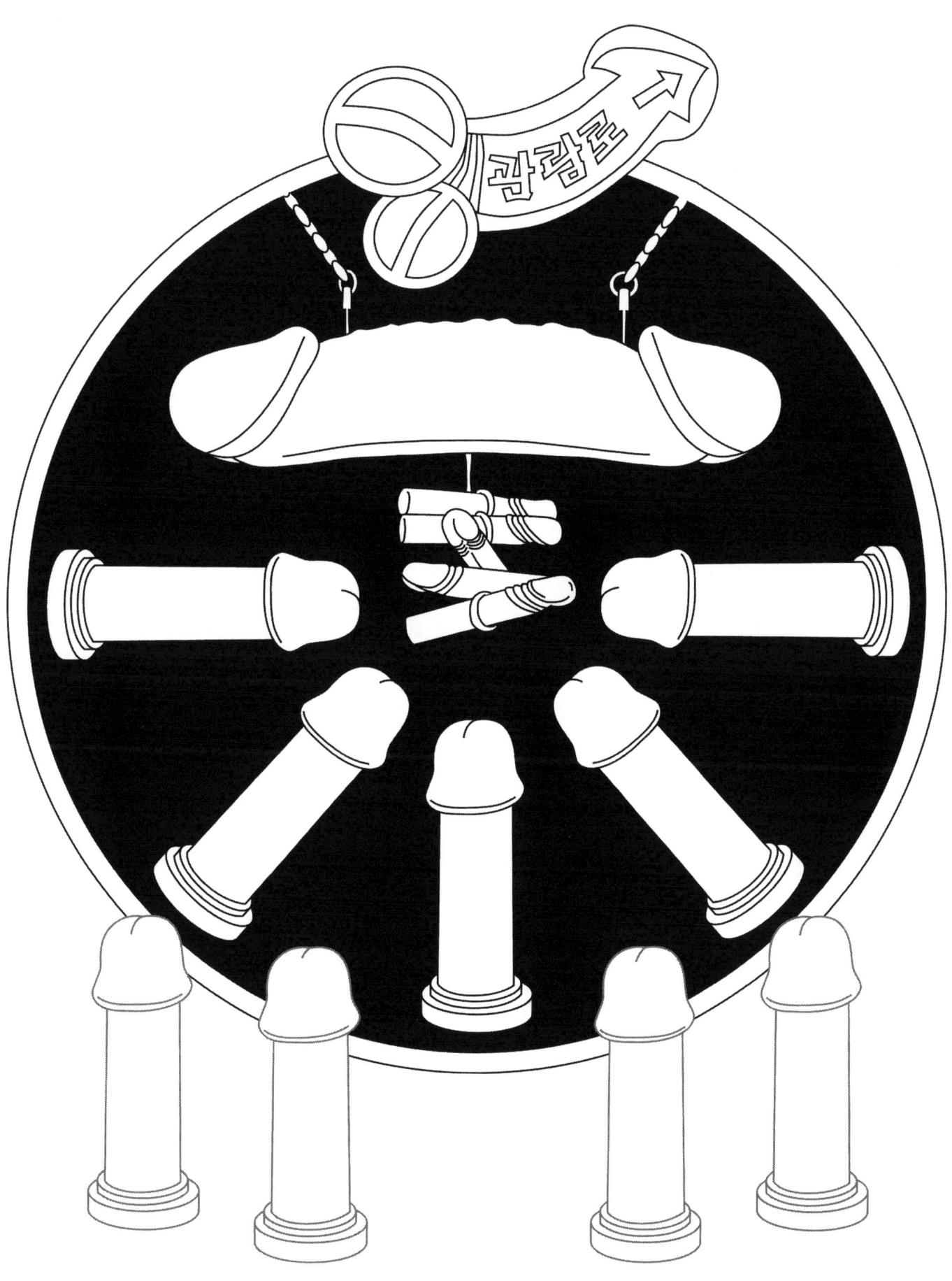

Roman bas relief

Phallic carving found at the amphitheatre at Nimes, France.

Depicting a Roman woman riding a winged triple phallus.

Aubrey Beardsley (1872 -1898)

Beardsley was a brilliant English illustrator
whose erotic and decadent ink drawings where
published in the notorious 'The Yellow Book'.

Beardsley was controversial in his day, and his dark
and grotesque images often featured
enormous penises.

Penis Mandala on Black

I have repeated the Penis Mandala as it looks great
on black.

Medieval Cock Ride

Illustration included in The Smithfield Decretals.
Part of an illuminated latin manuscript
created in Southern France c 1300.

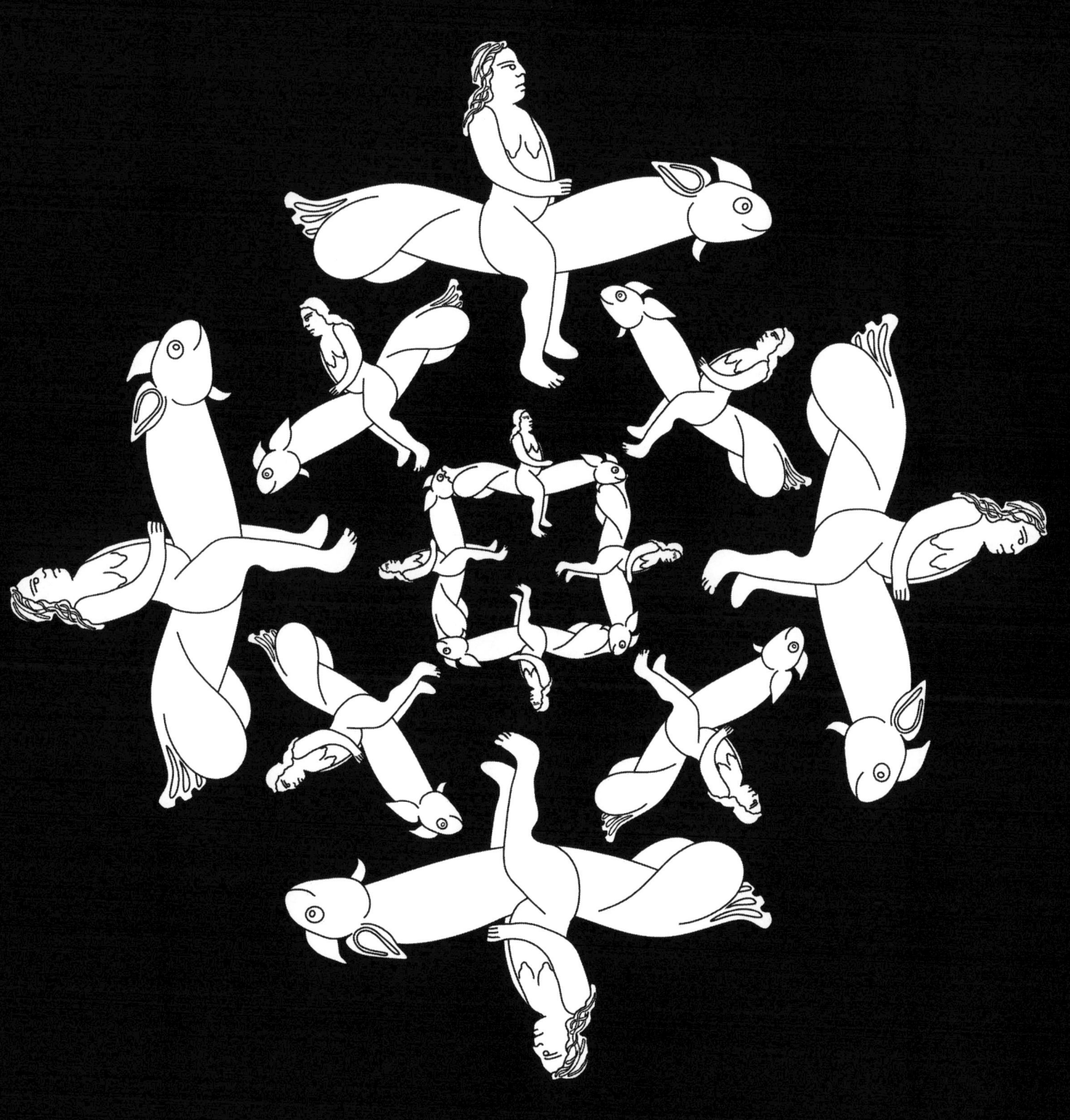

Roman Bell Cocks on black

More cocks with bells on.

Flower Cock on white

Leonardo Da Vinci
'Vitruvian Man'

The root of the penis in Leonardo's iconic draw-
ing, looking at ideal human geometric proportions,
starts at half the height of the man.

The Exedra of Dionysus
Delos Island, Greece

On the island are two pillars erected 300 B.C.
celerating Dionysos.
Each support a huge phallus.
Sadly the sculptures are now broken.
A central carving shows a cockerel whose head and
neck are elongated into a penis.

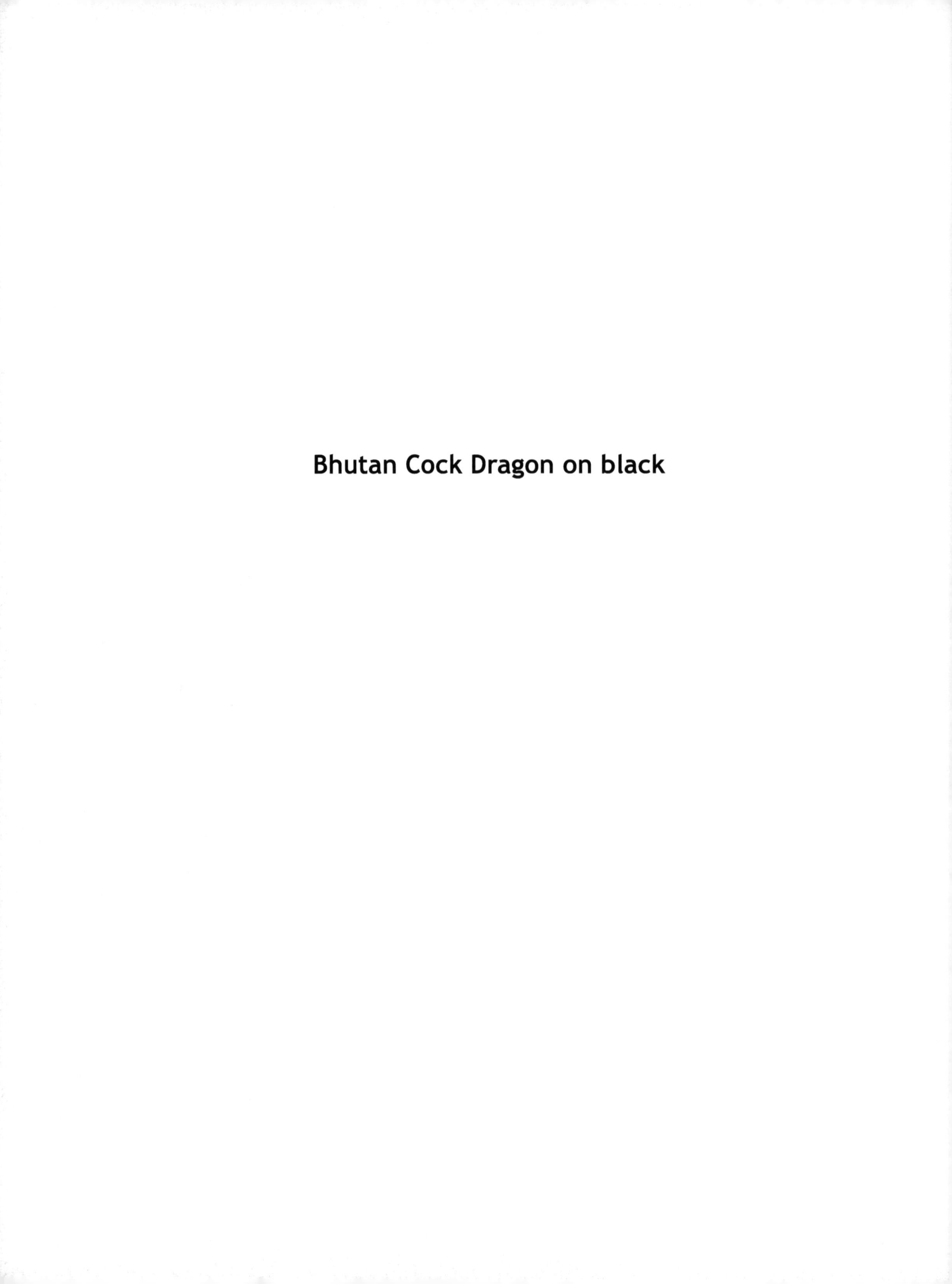

Bhutan Cock Dragon on black

Grecian Urn on black

Aubrey Beardsley (1872 -1898)

Beardsley wallpaper

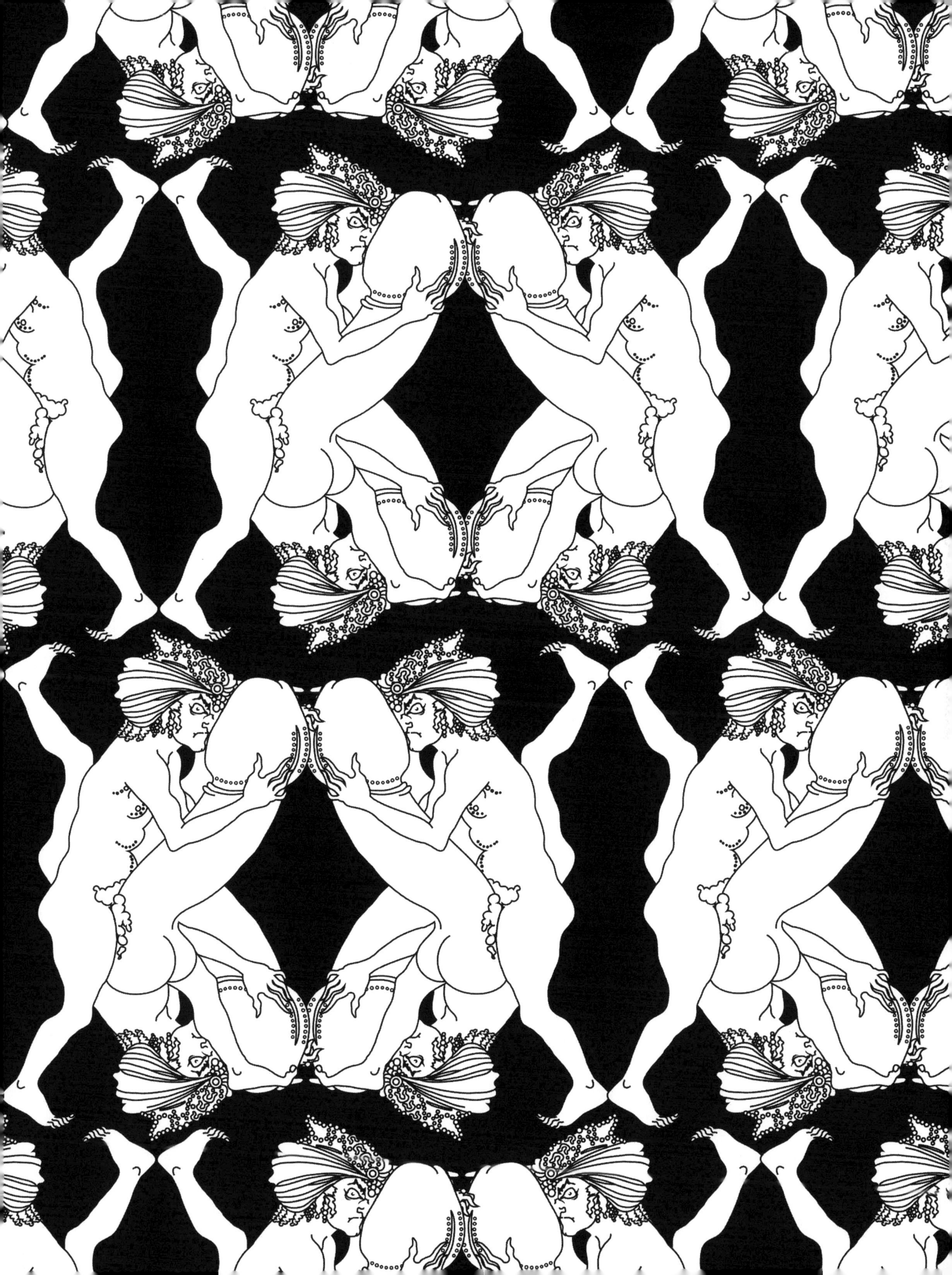

Nuns penis harvest on black

Michelangelo's David on black

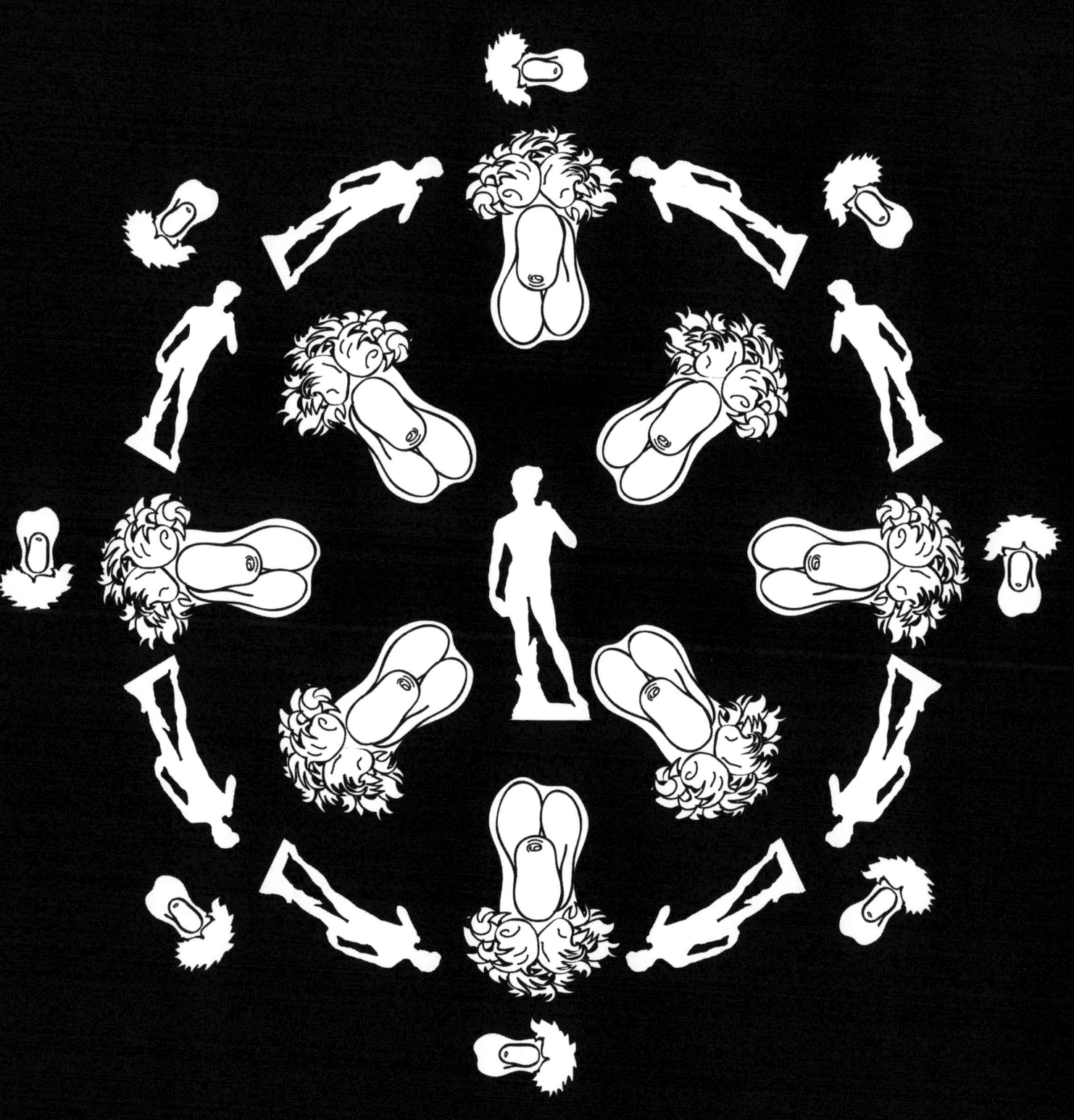

Egypt

Cocks and Osiris

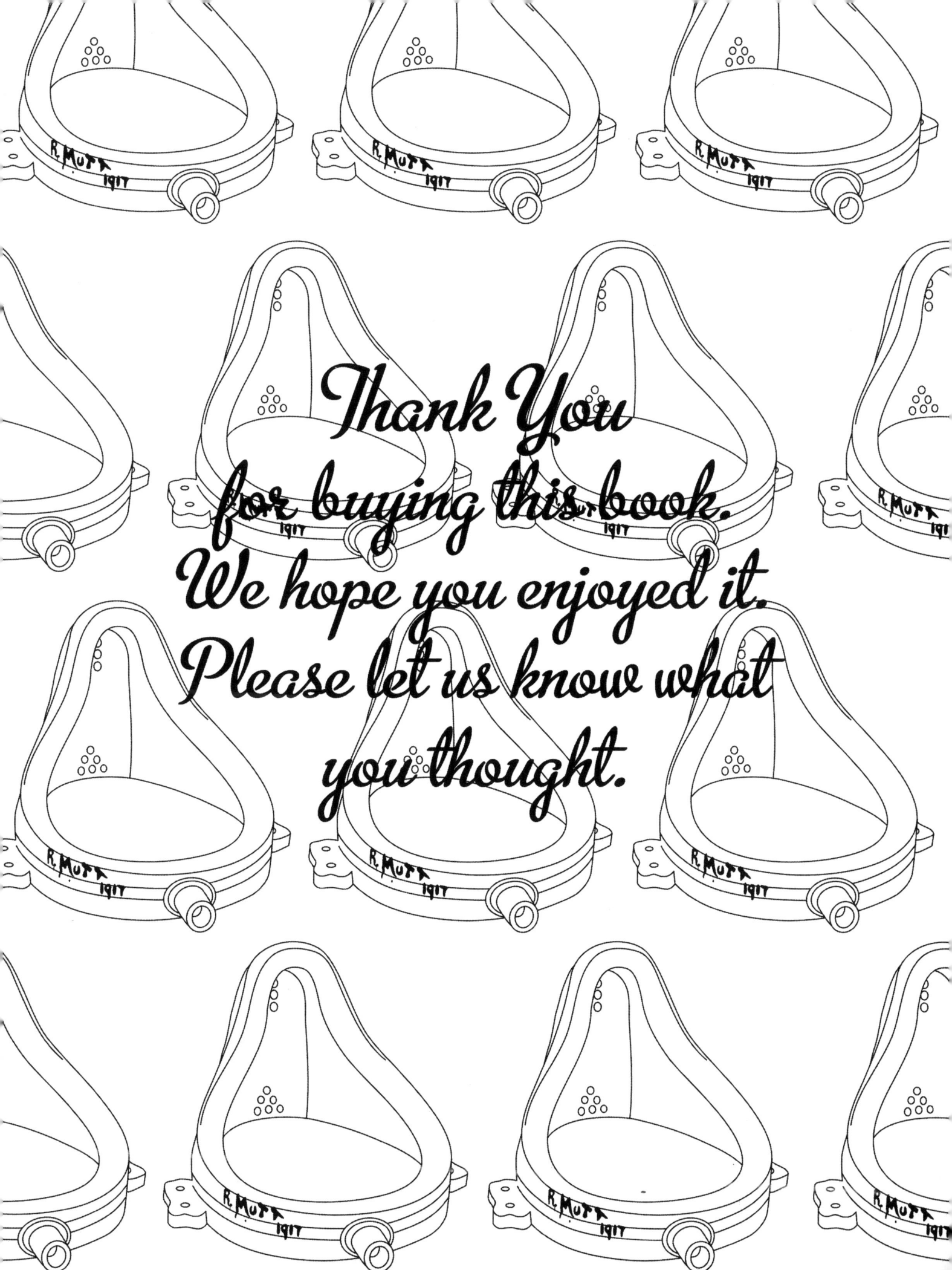

Thank You
for buying this book.
We hope you enjoyed it.
Please let us know what
you thought.

retroinc.co.uk

Thank you for purchasing this book.
We hope you enjoy it.

Please contact us with any comments you may have.
It's great to hear from readers.

We are running a competition to find readers favourite
Swear Words.
The winner gets to see theirs designed by Ella and will receive a
signed print of it and other goodies.

Find out more via our website or facebook page:
facebook.com/retroincbooks

Check out Ella's other adult colouring book on Amazon:

Colourful Swear Words - Entertaining Insults ISBN 978-09563290-97

Twitter @retrobooks
www.retroinc.co.uk